Living Geometries of Hope

ADRIANA VOLONA

VOLONA BOOKS

About the Author

By profession, Adriana Volona is a qualified mental health social worker, counsellor and group facilitator who has worked with disadvantaged women, men, and children in Australia, New Zealand and South Africa for the past 40 years. She currently provides counselling, as well as designing and delivering psycho-educational and therapeutic workshops for women who struggle with a variety of issues such as: domestic violence and dysfunctional relationships; dealing with depression, anxiety, and post-traumatic stress; grief and loss; problem anger; poor communication skills, childhood sexual, physical and emotional abuse; poor self-esteem and lack of confidence; parenting skills; change of life circumstances, and other traumatic experiences.

Adriana is also an artist and has a background in spirituality studies and practice. Some of her work, such as this book, are a blend of spirituality, her artwork and psychological well-being themes.

Title: *Living Geometries of Hope*

Author: Adriana Volona

ISBN: 978-1-7641936-0-3

Copyright   © July 2025 All rights are reserved.
                   No part of this book is to be reproduced or transmitted without written permission from the author.

Published by: Volona Books

Drawings: Drawing on book cover and all drawings featured on the right hand side pages of book are drawn by Adriana Volona.

Contributor: Paula Volona - Layout and Design
                   With special acknowledgment to Adobe Firefly for AI generated images used as part of the creative process in the composition of artwork for the left hand side pages, and the starry night background on cover of this book.
                   Bottom left hand side images on pp 16, 24, 32, 48 were photographs taken by Adriana Volona.

This book is dedicated
to our mother Maria Volona,
who inspired us to have hope

Preface

The concept of hope emerging from times of adversity has been around for centuries from all parts of the world. It seems to be an innate response of resilience in humanity.

From ancient times as far back as 1000BC, the Chinese Text: I Ching records: *"Peace replaces extreme evil."* Dr. Muata Ashby translates an ancient Egyptian proverb: *"Know thyself deathless and able to know all things, ... Think of thyself in all places at the same time, earth, sea, sky, not yet born, in the womb, young, old, dead, and in the after death state."* The Australian Aboriginal cultures dating back centuries have proverbs about hope: *"Learn from yesterday, live for today, hope for tomorrow,"* and *"Believe you can and hold firmly onto your dreams."*

From Europe, the famous quote: *"It is always darkest just before the day dawneth,"* was written by English theologian Thomas Fuller in 1650.

From a young Jewish girl Anne Frank who wrote in her diary during her experience of the Holocaust from 1942-1944: *"I see the world gradually being turned into a wilderness, I hear the ever approaching thunder, which will destroy us too, I can feel the sufferings of millions and yet, if I look up into the heavens, I think that it will all come right, that this cruelty too will end, and that peace and tranquility will return again."* Anne Frank also wrote: *"Where there's hope, there's life. It fills us with fresh courage and makes us strong again."*

In 2022 during the current war against Ukraine, president Volodymyr Zelenskyy addressed the European Parliament with the statement: *"Life will win over death, and the light will win over darkness."*

Hilary Tam, expert on sustainability is quoted saying: *"Hope beats fear every time,"* and a writer from New Zealand, Sr Mary Scanlon LCM, writes: *"Hope is a flower that casts a radiance about us; it can grow only on earth and blooms best in adversity."*

From South America, Chilean writer Isabel Allende wrote: *"We all have an unsuspected reserve of strength inside that emerges when life puts us to the test."* Mexican Artist Frida Kahlo has been recorded to have said: *"At the end of the day, we can endure much more than we think we can."*

From East Africa there is a proverb: *"To get lost is to learn the way,"* and from West Africa there is another proverb: *"The split tree still grows."* From South Africa, Nelson Mandela, is quoted to have stated: *"Remember that hope is a powerful weapon even when all else is lost."*

From the Middle East, Kahil Gibran wrote: *"Out of suffering have emerged the strongest souls,"* and *"The deeper that sorrow carves into your being, the more joy you can contain."* Rabbi Jonathan Sacks who wrote the book: *The Politics of Hope,* stated: *"Hope is the belief that, together, we can make the world better."* Syrian artist Alaa Al Khayat who escaped the war in Syria, painted his experience in an exhibition entitled: *"Finding Hope in the Midst of Adversity."* Writing about the horrors of the current war in Gaza, Pakistani journalist Nadeem Ahmed stated: *"In the heart of adversity, hope emerges as the strongest force for change,"* and *"Amidst the chaos, children in Israel and Palestine become the architects of a brighter, conflict-free world."* Palestinian poet Mosab Abu Toha, a survivor of war atrocities, writes: *"Palestinians love life. I can tell you about my father who planted some plants in our bombed garden, and he's eating some eggplant, some pepper, some cabbage. I mean, we are planting this hope next to the rubble of our bombed house."*

These quotes are only an infinitesimal smattering on the concept of maintaining hope in times of crisis as expressed in literature and the arts.

With so much material from most cultures on this subject in past and present times of struggle, why write more? In times of conscious suffering on a massive scale, emotional overwhelm can sometimes block our remembering that the sun does eventually penetrate dark clouds or rise after the darkness of the night. This book *Living Geometries of Hope* is another energetic addition to the Spirit of Hope in the human psyche. It is meant to be another ray amongst the countless rays of hope to reinforce resilience in the face of challenges.

Adriana Volona

Source of All
in us,
through us,
with us...

Source of All
in me,
through me,
with me...

The toughest labor pain
is just before
the birth of a child

Through time, the living
generate and propagate

The most parched drought
is just before
the monsoon rains

Through time, the living learn to
adapt

The greatest exhaustion
is just before
the finish line

Through time, the living develop
resilience

The hardest part of a problem
is just before
an effective solution arises

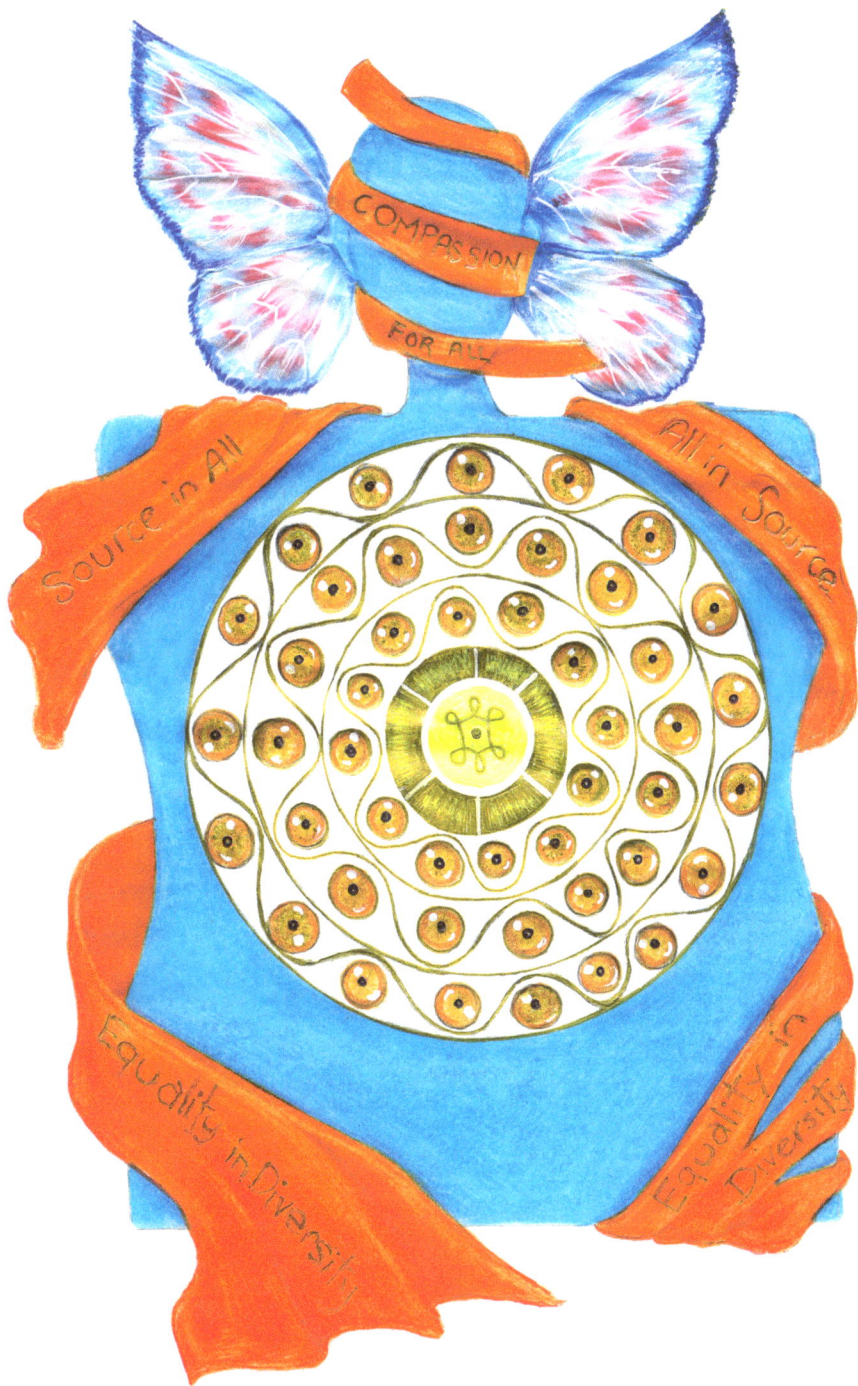

Through time, the living
explore and expand

The loneliest moment
is just before
an unexpected friendly contact

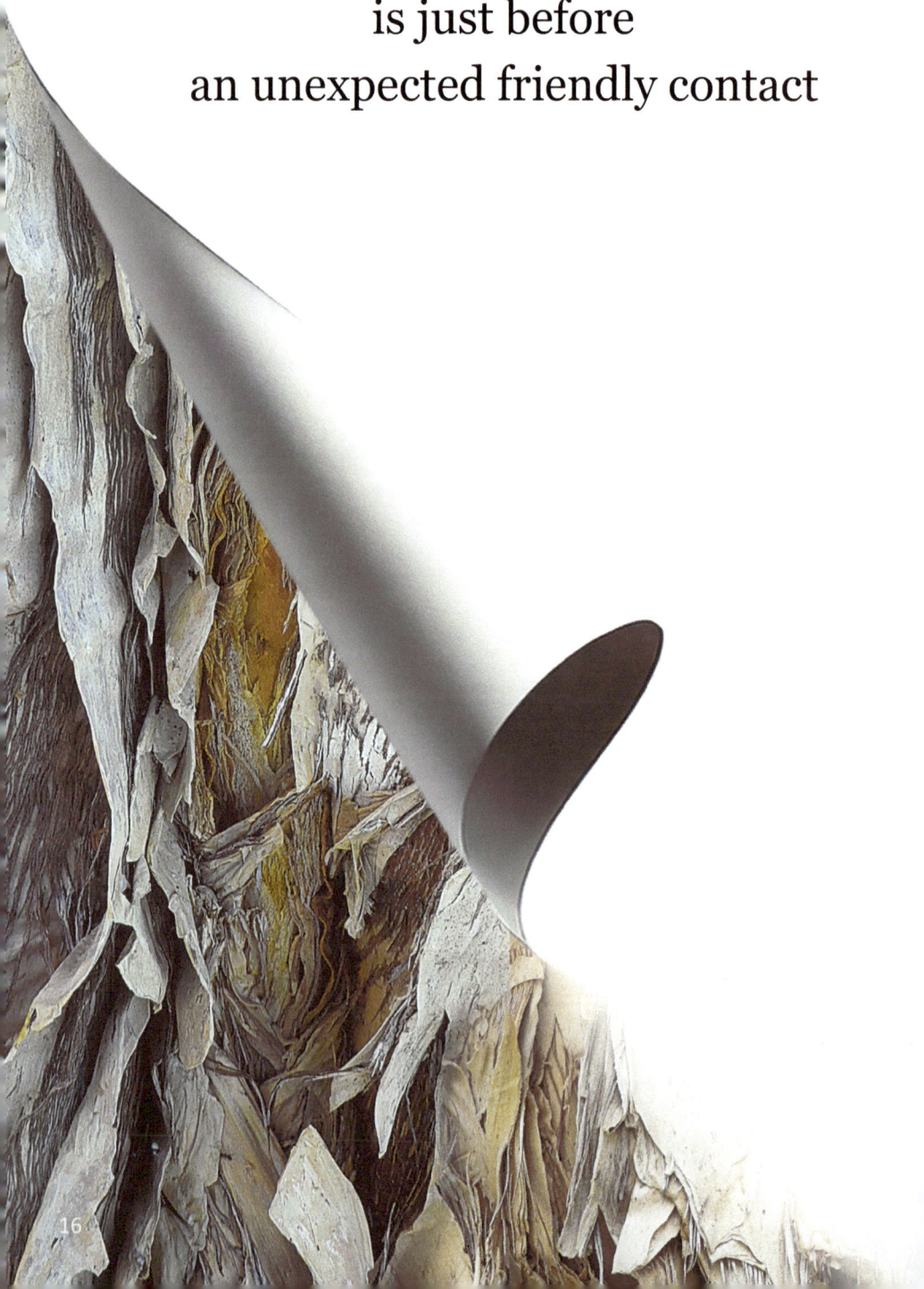

Through time, the living
gather together harmoniously

The instance you think:
'this is the end',
is just before
help arrives to save you

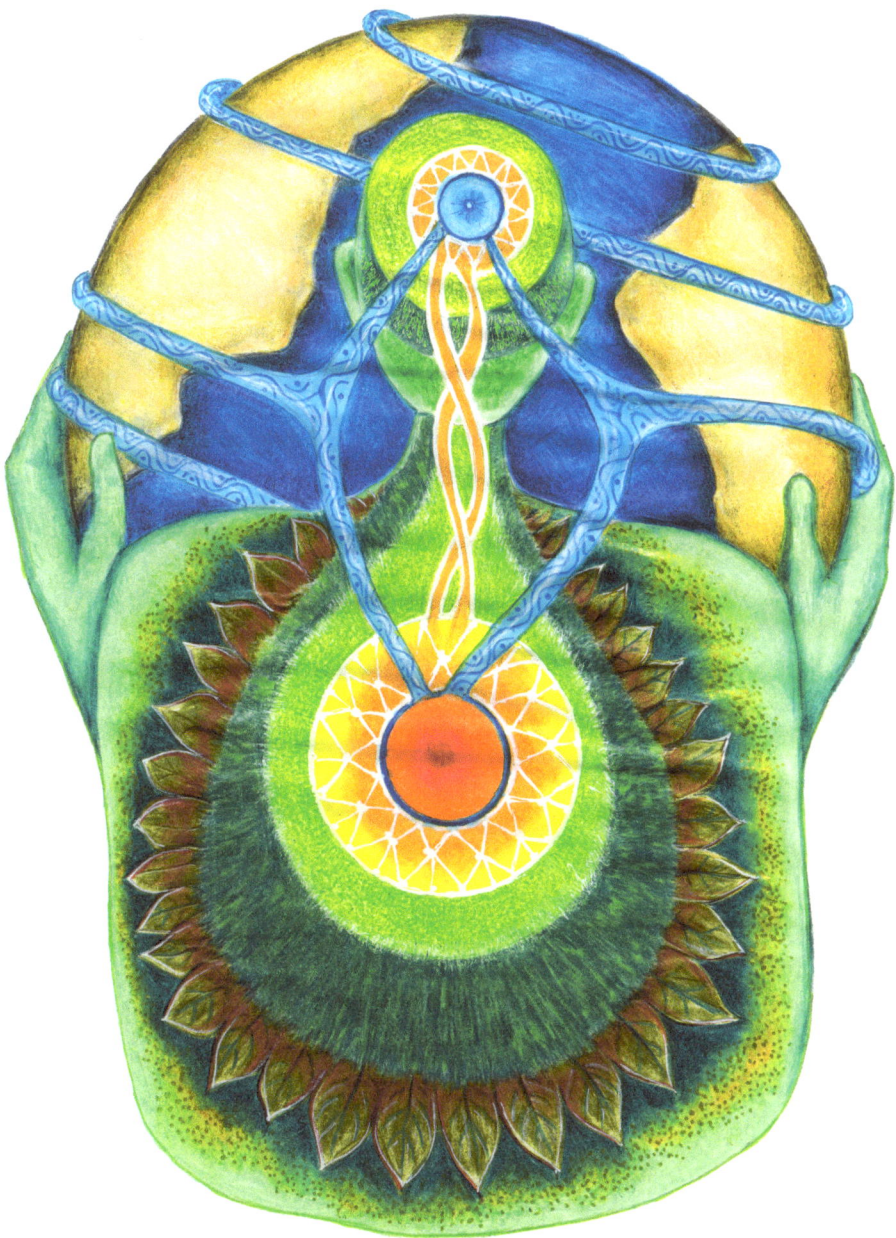

Through time, the living
are drawn towards their
interconnection

The severest time of captivity
is just before
freedom is achieved

Through time, the living
discover their equality

The anxious panic
is just before
the tolerable facts
are discovered

Through time, the living learn to
observe more acutely

The time you think you failed,
is just before
a new possibility arises

Through time, the living
evolve

The moment you are convinced
there is no other way,
is just before
another way opens

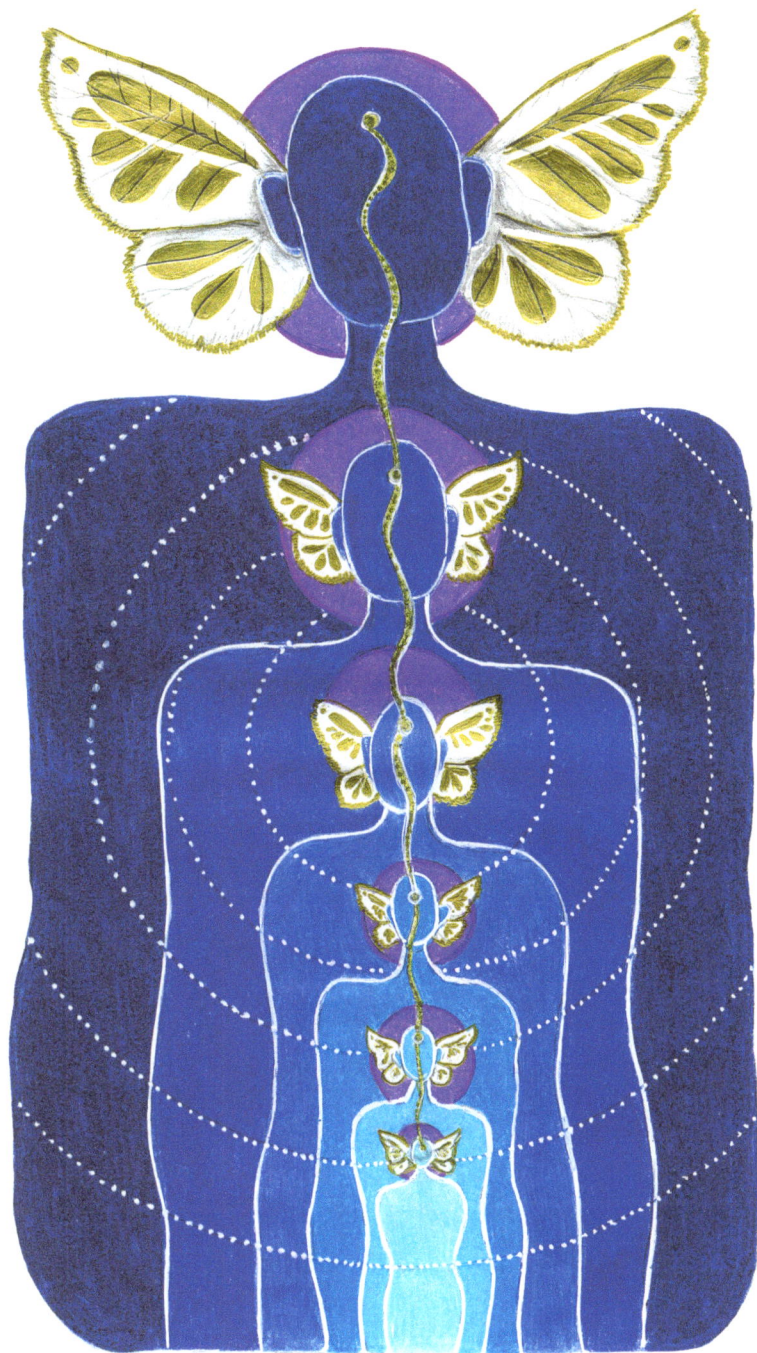

Through time, the living
unfold

The relentless temptation
to 'give up'
is just before
you reach your destination

Through time, the living
move

The most dogmatic insistence
of having the whole truth,
is just before
the realization that everyone
has only a part
of a contextualized truth

Through time, the living gain
insight and wisdom

The strongest feeling
of helplessness
is just before
turning the corner
to empowerment

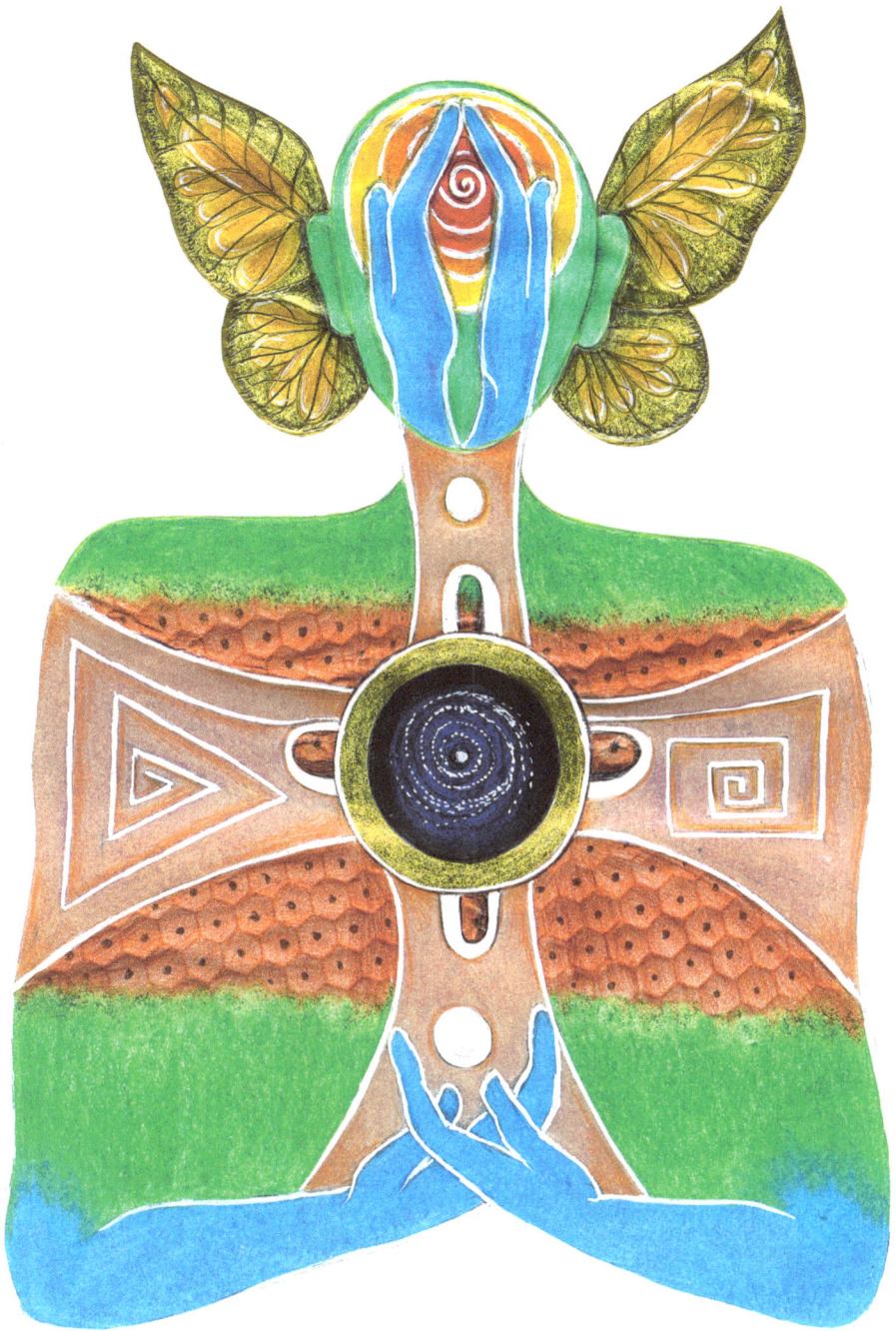

Through time, the living become more
aware of their consciousness

The strongest push against
'I can't',
is just before
the discovery of
'I can'

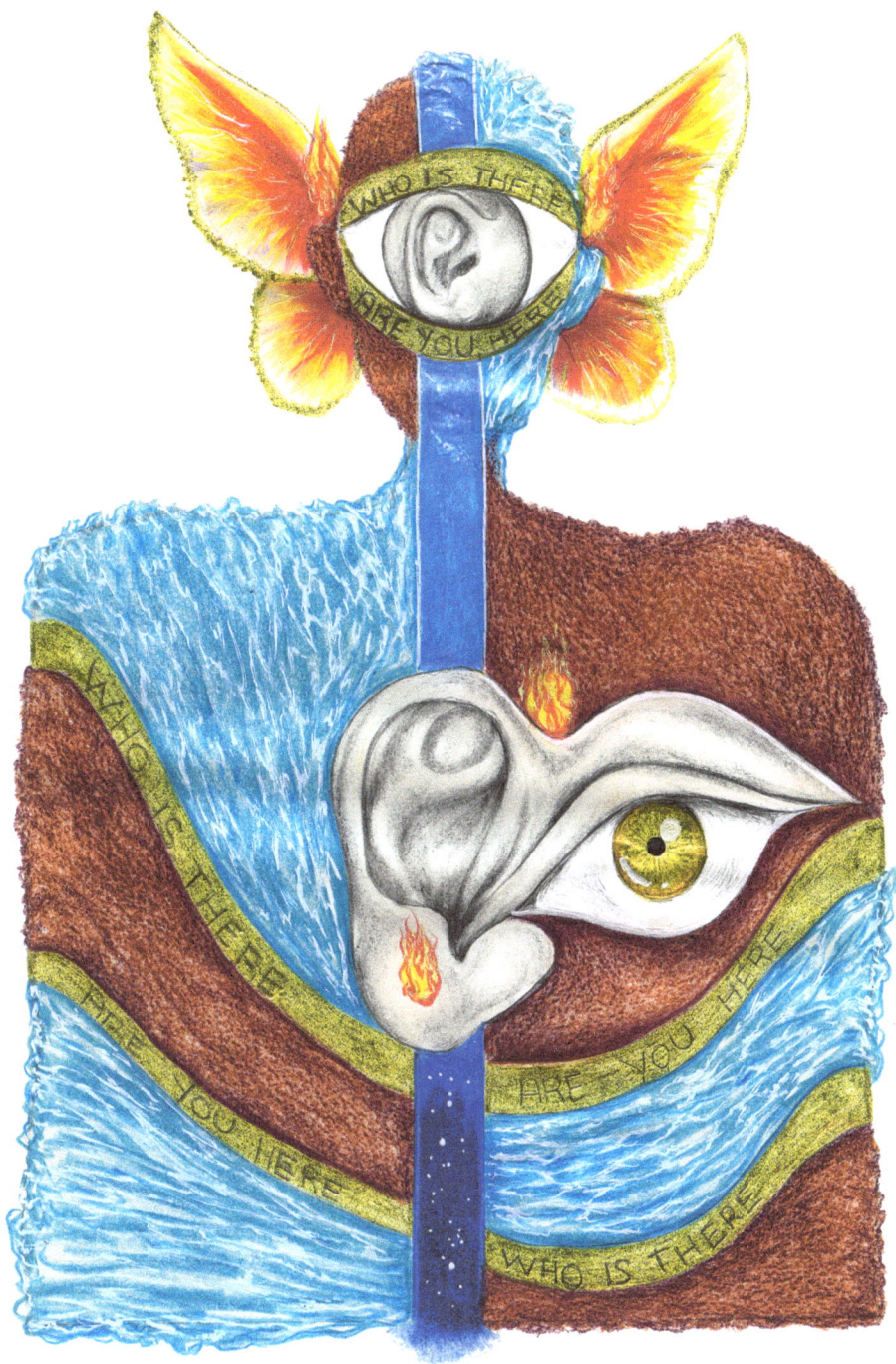

Through time, the living
transform

The most pressurizing urge to react
is just before
your value for harmony
illuminates you

Through time, the living learn to
respond gracefully

The loudest ridicule, mockery and insult of innovators and explorers
is just before
they are acclaimed
as geniuses and heroes

Through time, the living learn to
communicate more respectfully

The height of arrogance
is just before
the experience
of being in the shoes
of the most vulnerable

Through time, the living
grow

The unrelenting point
of resistance against oppression
is just before
the oppressed rise up
to claim their right to justice

Through time, the living learn how to
survive and thrive

The fiercest fight for
the 'survival of the fittest'
is just before
the awareness
that all the living
are interconnected

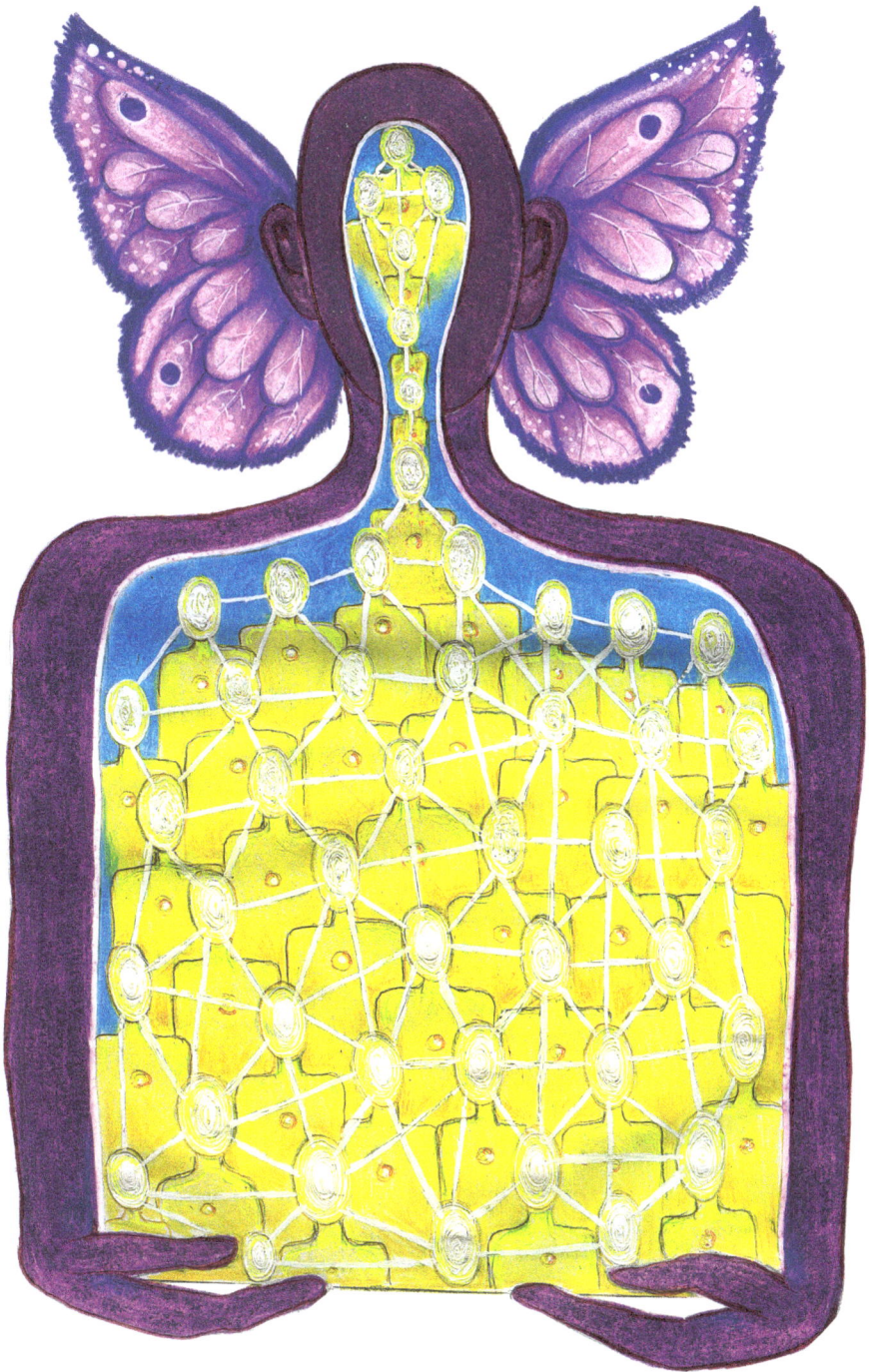

Through time, the living learn to
know the core of who they are

The worst nightmare
is just before
you wake up to find yourself
in a safe place

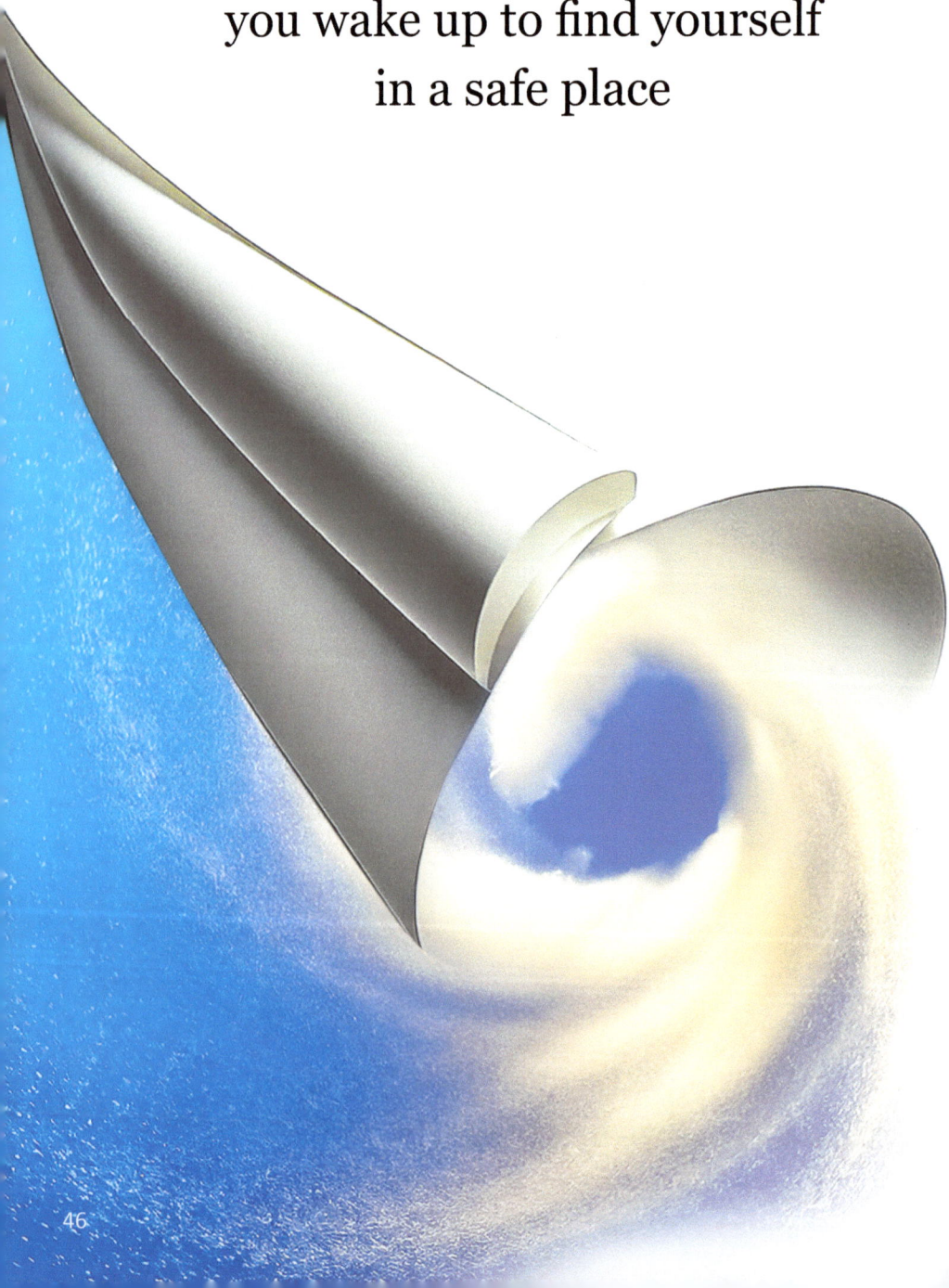

Through time, the living learn to
breathe more consciously

The harshest exclusion
of the unfamiliar
is just before
their acceptance and inclusion

Through time, the living learn to
love

The lowest point
in not having purpose
is just before
the understanding
that unconditional kindness
is the highest of purposes

Through time, the living understand why they
exist

The greatest terror of cowardice
is just before
discovering
the courage to act

Through time, the living
rise to better serve life

The extreme swing
to one direction
is just before
the pendulum moves
to the opposite direction

Through time, the living
Change

The furthest point
of disconnection
is just before
the spark of connection

Through time, the living
create beauty

The brightest stars in the sky are
just before
they extinguish and disappear.
Similarly, an era of corruption
and inequality is strongest
and on the way to decay
just before
a new era of inclusiveness,
harmony and justice rises.

Through time, the living
leave traces of their movements

www.ingramcontent.com/pod-product-compliance
Lightning Source LLC
LaVergne TN
LVHW010022070426
835508LV00001B/6

*9 7 8 1 7 6 4 1 9 3 6 0 3 *